CHINESE JOURNEY

CHINESE JOURNEY

Photographs by Gun Kessle

Text by Jan Myrdal

PANTHEON BOOKS

A Division of Random House   New York

First Printing

All rights reserved under International and Pan-American Copyright Conventions.
Published in New York by Pantheon Books, a division of Random House, Inc.,
and simultaneously in Toronto, Canada, by Random House of Canada Limited.
Manufactured by Amilcare Pizzi, Milan, Italy
under the direction of Chanticleer Press, Inc., New York

Library of Congress catalog card number: 65-15965

To Rune Hassner

CONTENTS

PREFACE

This book is no study. It is a record of the conscious and emotional responses of two European intellectuals making three journeys in China. The pictures are the most important part of the whole; my text is based on the diary I kept during these journeys. This is no "objective" description. It is personal. But not private.

The act of seeing seems to me more honest than the act of verbalizing — maybe because I do not see pictorially. I am a writer, a novelist, a reporter, a critic, a sociologist. Gun Kessle, my wife, is a painter, an etcher, a photographer. I have known her since we were children. We went to the same (suburban, middle-class) school in Stockholm during the war. Then she left for a TB sanatorium and I for a small-town newspaper. She came out of the sanatorium after some years, and went to London to study painting. I drifted over Europe, writing. She entered the Royal Academy school of fine arts in Stockholm. When I came from Paris in 1955 (during the Hungarian crisis), we met again. Then we left for Asia in a small 2 CV Citroën.

We seldom hold the same opinions. At least not at the same time. We change each other, but whether we understand each other when we discuss is doubtful. And so we have talked continuously since 1956. I do not have her eyes, can never see what she sees. She does not understand what I try to formulate. This continuity of divergence and change gives me at least a new dimension in my perception of reality.

Gun is a painter. I am a writer. Thus we are never simply the two of us when we are alone. We have been "alone" for nine years now, and there is always a third one along with us — the audience, the reader. He determines our way of perceiving. So three of us made these journeys. And this book itself becomes real to us only at the moment the reader reacts to it. Until that moment it is just a thing of paper, glue, and ink.

Between January, 1958, and January, 1963, we traveled in Asia. In April, 1962, we left India for China. During the first four years I wrote two books on Afghanistan and one novel.

Gun painted, drew, and took photos. We got the means to travel by making audio-visual educational material on Asia for schools.

Back in Sweden in the winter of 1960–61, we asked for visas to China. I wanted to do a "neutral" book, a factual, scholarly work on a Chinese village. That we got visas is not strange. We are Swedes; as such we can go anywhere we want. A small and neutral country that just wants to survive must have good relations with all the powers. China is one of them. We have an embassy in Peking, our trade is on the increase. In the Swedish travel agencies they sell tourist trips to China. And our government does not care where we go. The welfare state has a nineteenth-century liberal outlook. We went to China largely financed by the Swedish State Writers' Fund.

Our visas were valid for one year, but our money lasted only nine months. In China we were allowed journeys that then were "unusual." Later, as the economic situation improved, other journalists were given similar facilities. We were a kind of experiment. Here, then, is the record of our journeys.

Mythical beast, ceremonial road to Shih San Ling, the tombs of thirteen Ming Dynasty emperors outside Peking

We were in Delhi. Northern India was getting hot. It was April and our two-room flat in Defence Colony was stuffy. The fan was squeaking. I looked through the second draft of my book on India. I didn't like it. We had been in Asia for nearly five years, Gun Kessle and I. So I wrote my publishers that they would have to wait for a better year to get that book.

Gun said, "Let's go back to Herat. From there we could drive towards the Persian Gulf. Over Kerman and Sirjan to Bandar Abbas. It would be hot but interesting."

That afternoon I told the pensioned subahdar major who was our landlord that we were leaving. Gun was packing. I checked our car. In the morning we got a cable that our year-old application for Chinese visas had been granted. Such cables arrive in fiction. But in our case, this was the way it really happened. I cabled my publishers for money. Then I asked for permission to take the car to China.

"Sorry. Not allowed. Regulations."

I tried to book passage on a ship from Calcutta to Shanghai.

"Sorry, sir. There are no ships from Calcutta to Shanghai any more."

We flew to Hong Kong. There we bought two bicycles, and boarded a British ship for Tientsin. We were the only passengers.

"Nobody goes like that any more. They take the train or they fly."

The crew was Chinese. The officers were from Scotland and Northern Ireland.

"Occupied Ireland, mind you."

We took the train from Tientsin to Peking. There they found our bicycles.

"In fact, you are not allowed to have your own transport."

But they relented and we got permission to bicycle in Peking.

Guardians, Yuan Dynasty stone carvings (A.D. 1345)
inside the gate at Chuyuakuang Pass near Nankow

The children were of school age. The youngest were six years old. The balloons had been given them several hours ago. As they began marching in the parade, each one took hold of the string to his balloon with his left hand. The right was for waving. A tide of balloons running up Changan Avenue. As the children came to Tienanmen Square, they all let go of their balloons in front of the tribune at this Gate of Heavenly Peace where Mao Tse-tung and the other leaders greeted them. As the children marched away with empty hands, they were all smiling. Both leaders and children. Thousands of children smiling because they had given up their balloons. Rare toys that few have.

This description is ambiguous. Stressing the word "smiling" when describing how the children gave up their balloons, I evoke an emotion among many readers. If verbalized, this emotion would amount to saying that the children had been spiritually violated, been changed to "blue-clad ants." But this emotion is more relevant to that reader's culture (in which it is "unnatural" for a child willingly to give up a balloon for social reasons) than to the Peking scene that is described. Today, as in former times, Chinese culture is dominated by ideas of social morality and social control.

Conversely this emotion determines the spontaneous Chinese reactions to the social phenomena of Western countries. The immediate reaction of both the mandarin of 1850 and the *kanpu* (administrator of the organized revolution) of 1965: Westerners are faceless inhabitants of a social jungle, obeying the laws of the jungle and not those of a civilized community.

Even aside from the social revolution in China and the political conflict, this in itself renders the dialogue difficult.

And today the Chinese leaders regard themselves as the spokesmen not only of civilization but also of the poor and oppressed, the insulted and humiliated, against the high and the mighty, the few, the barbarians.

Think of the Swedes. Double their number. Multiply by five. Write that sum down in figures. Put another zero at the end. That makes 700,000,000. These are the Chinese. The actual figure might be 50,000,000 higher or lower. In official documents the Chinese say, "We 650,000,000 Chinese . . ." In this void of uncertainty the number of all Frenchmen in the world would get lost and there would still be room in which to lose several minor nationalities of Europe.

Take the history of the United States. Start with the foundation of Jamestown in 1607. Then count the years. Let the years be seconds. Look at the clock. Six minutes have passed. Take the history of China. Start with the Shang Dynasty from which there are written documents (albeit in the form of oracle bones). That makes about 3,600 years. Then look at the clock again. Feel the difference between six minutes and one hour.

These are not drawing-room games. They are Peking hotel-room games as the wind blows and the dust from Gobi covers books and papers and cameras. Sensing the proportions.

Also perspectives differ. Visiting an old professor I knew in Peking (we had discussed Strindberg as a Sinologist, and Professor Liu had shown me a rare edition of Strindberg's *The Roots of the Chinese Language*) I saw his grandson reading. I asked what the boy read. He said, *"The Romance of the Three Kingdoms."*

The heroes were from the third century. The book was first printed in 1494. The novel had for centuries furnished examples and models to ordinary Chinese but also to the peasant leaders of the Ming Dynasty rebellions, to leaders of the Taiping Rebellion . . . and to the young Mao Tse-tung.

He ordered the guards to take Kuan Yu out and kill him.

For friendship's sake he risked death.

Men yet unborn will admire his gallantry.

To know what became of Kuan Yu, you must read the next chapter.

17

Our Chinese visas were valid for one year. But we stayed only nine months. Then we took the train towards Stockholm. The third journey in China: the Burma Road through Yunnan had taken our last funds and we could just scrape together enough money to buy our ticket for the Trans-Siberian Railroad.

As our time was short and China large, we had chosen to leave out most of central China and the cities on the coast. We concentrated on making three inland journeys. On the second of them we wanted to stay in a village, live with the peasants, and try to get an understanding of the peasant revolution. This we had already stated in the visa application.

We made our first trip to Inner Mongolia. (What was happening to the Mongols? What was becoming of the nomads?) We made our second trip from Loyang to Yenan. We lived in a village in North Shensi. We made our third trip through Yunnan from Kunming to the Burma border. (We had been on the other side of that border two years earlier.)

We were interested in people. For Gun it is seeing and depicting. Whatever material she uses to "see" with — oil, copper, gouache, photographic film — her angle remains the same. People in human surroundings. Neither heroes nor criminals. Never living examples to prove a thesis. I tried to see the pattern of change and continuity half a generation away from the victory of the revolutionary peasant armies. Coming from South Asia, I was specially interested in the (somewhat intangible) if and how of national integration in China. This volume is thus a combination of our methods of seeing. There are others. And as the Dominican Father Gaspar da Cruz stated in the introduction to his treatise on China, 1596:

I also hereby give readers a necessary warning by which they can conjecture the greatness of the things of China; i.e., that although distant things often sound greater than they really are, this is just the opposite, because China is so much more than it sounds and the sight of it makes a very different impression from what is heard and read about it, as has been verified by myself and others after we have seen the things of China.

Columns and beams, upper hall of bell tower, Sian. Tang foundation,
Ming building, restored under Ch'ing Dynasty, again restored 1952

INNER MONGOLIA

We were in the Silingol League of Inner Mongolia. There stood three yurts in the valley. We arrived at dusk and a cold wind blew over the grasslands. A smell of rain hung in the air. During the last miles the track had gone through salty marshes. Here under the hills began the good grazing land.

Our host that evening was named Renchen, his wife Kandima. Renchen was a man about thirty-five years old. Spoke slowly and deliberately. He had a worn brown *kalat* and riding boots of leather. When he smiled, it showed only in the corners of his eyes. There was a wolf skin inside the door of the yurt. The yurt seemed poor and the felt carpets were worn.

"This is not a good year," said Renchen. "The frost was hard, the snow frozen, spring came late. Quite a number of our animals died. We have two natural enemies here. The weather and the wolf. There is nothing much to do about the weather, but you can always kill the wolf."

"Renchen is a wolf hunter," said Amin Bokha, the party secretary.

"Wolf hunter," said Renchen. "Wolf hunter — well, I kill a wolf now and then. I get prize money for that from the state. Ten yuan for a large one, five for a cub. The skin one can keep or sell. Once the party suggested that this prize money should go to the collective, but now they have changed their opinion."

"That was a deviation," said the party secretary.

"He who kills a wolf kills it. That's the way I see it. I took six wolves this year. There are not so many of them any more. During the disorder, after the war and the liberation, they came in packs. Then they took people, too. To hunt wolf? You drive him. You ride after him until he gets tired. You just keep behind him, to the left of him. It is important to keep the distance just right. When you feel that he is tired you ride up beside him and crack him over the muzzle. He just tumbles and falls and you finish him off with a knife. That is all. It is just a question of the right moment."

20

We sat in the yurt, eating meat and drinking strong local alcohol. ("We make it collectively at the state farm. That makes it cheaper.")

Renchen said, "When I was young, I was poor and life was hard. The only joy I had in life was drinking. When I was drunk, I was happy. But then people swindled me. And when I woke up next morning, life was again just as it always had been."

Kandima came in from the night outside. It was raining. She sat down near the entrance. She looked at us while we were talking and drinking, then she went out once more, came back, fed the fire with dried dung, and stirred the large milk pot. It was hot inside the yurt, and the air was heavy with the smell of men and boiling milk and burning *argol*.

I looked at Renchen and remembered the young official in Peking saying, "All the Mongol herdsmen are now being settled in houses." I had not believed him then. I had tried to argue. Nomadism is not a question of "bad habits." It is an adaptation to extensive grazing.

"We move about six times a year," said Renchen.

In Silinhot town I had talked with Hu Shing-ga, the vice-director of the Silingol League. An old kanpu from the northwest (with blue eyes), who had been directing the work here since 1948.

When I asked him about houses, he said, "We build towns. In these towns we build houses. We build administrative centers in the different people's communes. There are houses. For the people, the herdsmen, we try to get real yurts. Many lived formerly in tents only. A house, you see, is cheaper than a good yurt. But yurts are necessary as long as grazing is our chief industry. The two great changes in the construction of yurts have been a folding chimney tube that can be packed along with the yurt when moving — it makes the air in the yurt better, thus lessens eyestrain and the rate of tuberculosis — and folding wooden floors that isolate the yurt from the frozen ground and protect the herdsmen against rheumatism."

Inside yurt of Mijik

Young woman, Bayan Bolkha;

Tankto, the singer

So, it would well be possible for me to sit in the yurts, drink horse-milk wine, feel the continuity with former centuries, and formulate my impression of the wine in the words of William of Rubruck, a traveler who has been dead nearly seven hundred years: "Cosmos . . . gladdens the soul, yet it makes a weak head confused." I drank the kumiss and it was a sourish freshness on my tongue. And while the Han kanpus looked skeptically at us, Botech and I swore brotherhood. Stood up. Kissed each other. Exchanged knives. He got my Mora sheath-knife and I got his dagger ("Made by our own blacksmith"). And the knives were wrapped in *tchaddaks* of silk and we were brothers. In the morning my head was heavy. My eyes smarted when I went out in the sun.

This is true, though romantic. A simplified truth. Thus a lie. There behind the seat of honor in Renchen's yurt should have been the altar. Now a big and new alarm clock shone with nickel instead. Over the clock was a picture of Mao Tse-tung.

The clock was bought in the co-op, and Renchen earned a salary on the state farm.

"My wife earns money, too."

But in another yurt, another night, Tankto the old man was singing with a high-pitched voice, tears trickling down his cheeks.

"It is a song about love," says his son. "But it can also be a song about the poor and despised. It is a song about longing, about him who is long gone. But it can also be a song about horses. It is a song about a sister, but it can also be a song of a bride. It all depends on how you feel. He is a poet. His language is so intricate and beautiful."

Old men still sing in the yurts. But if that is the criterion of nationhood — to prize singing and popular art — Sweden has not been a nation since the end of the last century.

Renchen says, "I saw the clock and I asked: 'What is the price?'"

Mijik, his family and friends, drinking

Young herdsman, Bayan Bolkha

Mongol children playing

Milking the mare

Evening in the camp

(Overleaf) The young party secretary

29

Making tea in the yurt;
Mongol child, children's home, Huhehot

Mongol life in its traditional form has all the trappings of a romantic stereotype: there are wide open spaces, horses, hard riding, hard drinking, singing in the yurts, wrestling games, comradeship among men, and epic poetry.

The romantic sheen of this life fades if to that is added hunger, dirt, and illness. Small-pox, cholera, rheumatism, intestinal parasites, and all the other scourges of poverty the Mongols shared with the Hans. But there was a difference. Syphilis was endemic in the Mongol population; the rate was about 60 per cent.

The roots of that difference were social and not medical. From the point of view of health and mortality, one of the most striking differences between the Mongols and the Hans in Inner Mongolia was that the Mongols were syphilitic and there was no undue mortality of their female infants, while the Hans were not unduly syphilitic but their female infants tended to die very easily.

In the classical Han marriage system, girls became a burden — to bear a girl was bad luck. The Mongol morality on the other hand made women freer, made them valuable, placed very little importance on virginity and faithfulness in the purely sexual sense. The morality of the Mongols (disparaged by so many European travelers) was of the same type as that of the traditional Swedish, or Bavarian, or North English peasant society.

One of the truly great things done after the new regime took over is the virtual elimination of syphilis. Through three large campaigns syphilis has now been brought under control. Which also leads to a rising birth rate among the Mongols.

But this is also a part of a revolution in Mongol life that is greater than that of the introduction of Lamaism in the sixteenth century. Not only the sheen, also the reality of that life which William of Rubruck described is now fading and disappearing.

For the syphilis I feel no nostalgia whatsoever.

The temple at Bayan Bolkha, the Rich Fountain of the Western Banner of the Uchumuchin Tribe of the Silingol League, seems ancient. But it is only about sixty years old. It was built at the end of the Ch'ing Dynasty.

Visiting the Bayan Bolkha People's Commune, we walk from the new administrative barracks to the temple. The local kanpus say that it is without interest. When we open the creaking wooden doors, the Mongol kanpus stay outside. There used to be two hundred monks here. Now there are thirty-three.

"They are unreformed. They do not co-operate."

The yard is filled with debris. The temple is in need of repair.

"We have not managed to reach an agreement with the monks. If they make an agreement with us, they will get funds for repairs. They have funds of their own, of course. They say there is no need for repairs. But the roof has been mended. Some day we will reach an understanding. Then there will be a complete architectural restoration."

"Temples are monuments, a national heritage. This one will be restored as such when we reach an understanding."

When we leave the temple, people are looking at us. One of the Mongols from the People's Commune — not a kanpu, just an ordinary party member — says, "It was a pity you visited the temple. It gives them higher status. It was not necessary."

On the hill above the Peitze Temple in Silinhot is an *obo*, a cairn of stones. Older than the temple, much older. A cult place of Mongol shamanism. Then taken over by the Lamaist church. Now I see there new rags offered to the gods. The *obo* has been restored.

"That was done with government funds. It is a national monument."

Standing beside the *obo*, I see the temple and beyond the temple the new administrative buildings. This is not accidental. The pattern has a history.

Unreformed monks, Bayan Bolkha

The obo, Silinhot

In Peitze Temple, Silinho.

Central square, Silinhot town

Changing tire, main road north of Silinhot;
Kanpus and jeeps
in "kanpu center" of Silinhot

It's a day's drive from the town of Bayan Olhot down to Silinhot. The jeep rolls, jumps, and twists through the choppy grassland. Far away, other tracks. Now and then we stop. Two times we change tires. We shoot at big birds. I don't recognize them. After the midday meal we lie in the blue grass. The jeep, this small group of people (the driver and the interpreter sleep, they snore), a cluster of specks under a tiny white cloud.

Gun says, "I would like to stay here. It is such a wonderful landscape to paint, because it is so difficult. The shifting light, the changing colors, and the faraway herds."

I remember thinking, "At least this means that the political situation here is rather stable. The authorities are not afraid that we will be shot at."

This is evident. I know at first hand only what I have seen. And Inner Mongolia is an area nearly twice as large as France. Whether we would have been shot at in other regions I don't know. But there is a pattern I believe I see correctly. Part of it is constituted by the *obo,* the temple, and the new administrative buildings.

The Lamaist church was established in a national and religious revival at a time when it seemed possible that the Mongols and not the Manchus would attain power over China. Later on it was used also by the Manchus — the Ch'ing Dynasty — to keep control over the Mongols. The church with its temples and houses, its monks and herds, was a new factor in the nomad culture of the Mongols.

The People's Communes, the new towns, the new centers grow up around the nuclei formed by the temples (and princely mansions). There, a continuity. The temples have lost much of their power and wealth. But not all. They still own herds. And when the monks reform and co-operate ("When we monk masses rose against oppression," as a monk in Peitze Temple put it), they regain both prestige and a certain economic power (as in the temple carpet-factory in Silinhot). In this perspective the settling of the Mongol nomads becomes a long historical process.

(From top to bottom)
Cartwheel workshop, Bayan Olhot
Blacksmiths, Bayan Olhot
Bicycles of monks and employees of
Peitze Temple Carpet Factory, Silinhot

Herdsmen in the Consumers' Co-operative Store
of Bayan Bolkha People's Commune

But there is another aspect. At the Silinkalat stock-breeding farm, the director had said, "We came here in October, 1950. We were 22 men with 12 yurts and 1,022 head of cattle. Now we are 2,350 men and we have 120,000 head of cattle. It's a good land."

"You came. Was it empty?"

"Oh, yes. Some Buryat Mongols had been living here for some time. They had fought against the Soviet power in Siberia during that revolution. Then they had been in Outer Mongolia and fought there. They took this land thirty years ago. They worked with the Japanese army. They fought the People's Liberation Army. Then they lost and went away."

"Where to?"

"I don't know. That was before my time."

War, civil war, social revolution — even when all that is taken into account, the social and economic advances on the grasslands of Inner Mongolia are undisputable. The Mongols are once more increasing. From an estimated 1,470,000 in 1928, their number fell to about 800,000 in 1947. In 1962 they were 1,210,000. The Mongol future in Inner Mongolia thus is rosy. Or . . . ?

Inner Mongolia is a part of China. In 1953 the population of Inner Mongolia was 7,390,000. In 1957 it was 9,200,000. In 1962 it was 11,710,000. The number of Mongols increases. But they are a minority in their own land. A minority whose relative strength is decreasing. This is an old historical problem. It is not just a simple one of "Hanification." The Great Wall of China was designed both to keep the nomads out and the agriculturalists in. But the lands between the wall and the desert were through the centuries contested between the pastoralists and the agriculturalists.

The monks of Peitze Temple blow their long copper trumpets. A part of the ritual of a church that, by founding temples which grew to towns, began to change the Mongolian landscape four hundred years ago.

Reformed monks of Peitze Temple, Silinhot,
blowing copper trumpets

Backyard of Peitze Temple, Silinhot.
The temple carpet-factory

41

Morning calisthenics, Silinkalat
state stock-breeding farm

Salt caravan for Peking, Silinkalat
state stock-breeding farm

The wall had once marked the geographically possible limit of classical Chinese agricultural techniques. Later, under the Manchu emperors of the Ch'ing Dynasty it was a politically necessary boundary between two parts of their empire that were to be kept separate. The Manchus, ruling over the Han multitudes of China, needed the Mongol princes and warriors as allies against a possible rebellion of the Han population. Even intermarriage was forbidden.

But shortly before the turn of the century, when the Manchu power was crumbling, this policy could no longer be enforced, and the application of agricultural techniques that had been utilized in breaking up the American prairie led to the extension of agriculture northwards.

Between 1872 and 1923 the farmland frontier (with villages and ditches and roads) advanced at the rate of a mile a year. According to the figures of 1924 the breaking up of the Mongol pastures gave a 40 per cent yearly return on the original investment. The Han agriculturalists came not in thousands but in hundreds of thousands. The Mongols were poor and ill; their princes were selling the pastures (an unthinkable deed, according to Mongolian traditions); the herdsmen lost their lands. The Mongols were pushed further out on the marginal grazing lands at the border of the desert.

Now at the Silinkalat stock-breeding farm there are 2,260 men working. Of them 520 are Mongols, 1,710 are Hans, 23 are Hueis (Moslems), 5 are Manchus, and 2 are Koreans. And even far out on the grasslands at the Bayan Bolkha People's Commune, where there were virtually no Hans thirty years ago, there are now 421 Hans out of a total population of 1,622. (Two are Russians, by the way: "Recent immigrants. A man and his sister who crossed the border, applied for Chinese citizenship, and settled here.")

This is the problem of Inner Mongolia. And at Bayan Bolkha I saw good potato land. It just was waiting to be broken up.

Young pioneers visiting new city park, Huhehot

Out on the grasslands we had been sitting in the yurts, eating meat while the fat ran down our fingers. In Peking there was then nearly no meat. Here there were no vegetables. Yet in Peking this year there were plenty of vegetables. (During the bad years there had been hunger even in Peking. People had been really hungry. So hungry that they had to fall back on the old Chinese survival method of boiling tree leaves for food.)

This was not due to lack of organization. It was due to difficulties of transport. From Bayan Bolkha there were 360 miles of rough trails over prairie and desert to the nearest railhead. It was as difficult to bring the meat out as to bring goods in.

"Our problems are real," said Wang Tsai-tien in Huhehot. He was the party secretary of the Inner Mongolian Autonomous Region.

"We need an east-west railroad. It is absolutely necessary. For livestock breeding, agriculture, and industry. But a railroad means a large capital investment. The funds of our country are very limited. There is always a choice. We have discussed it. Maybe we will have to wait two, even three five-year plans. There is so much that is needed. And from the viewpoint of the country as a whole, we have no priority."

Despite the lack of funds Inner Mongolia is going through a period of deep change. The nomad economy is giving way to agriculture and industry.

So, even if the statement of the young official in Peking that "the Mongol herdsmen are being settled in houses" was factually untrue, it nonetheless was correct. The nomad culture is being changed to a settled culture. This will be a difficult and, for many, a painful adjustment.

There are more interpretations than one of what my friend Wu Tung, the normally abstinent poet from Peking, said to me when we had been drinking heavily of the kumiss in the yurt of Mijik:

"You are a guest. You don't have to drink. I am a Han, a kanpu. I must drink. I have to show respect for the traditions of the nationalities."

46

Craftsman in boot factory, Silinhot

(From top to bottom)
Workers in boot factory, Silinhot
Workers in textile mill, Huhehot
Textile mill, Huhehot

Workers in textile mill, Huhehot

49

Children playing, day nursery, Huhehot

The rationale of Chinese policy in Inner Mongolia is to effect this social, economic, and cultural change in order to fully utilize the rich soil and great natural resources of the region (which means the settling of some millions of Hans there) without getting a new flare-up of the national clashes between Mongols and Hans that marked the thirties. This explains both the relative abundance of consumer goods in the shops far out in the grazing area (despite the forbidding transportation costs), the protected position of the temples, the relatively favored position of the old "leading strata" of the Mongols, and the care that is taken to avoid hurting Mongol national pride. Personally, I see the celebrations in honor of Genghis Khan in this context and not in that of world politics.

The ethnic map of this part of Inner Asia is being remade. And that is an irrevocable historical change. Fields do not turn into grazing land.

Despite the beautiful new yurts the Mongol nomadic culture is doomed. But lest we become too sentimental on this score, let us keep in mind that so is the Lapp nomadic culture in Sweden. Whether this also means the end of Mongol nationality is another question. Nationhood is not just a specific form of economy and dress.

The Mongols are becoming integrated in China. They will not be Hans but Chinese. The new towns growing up around the old temples have hospitals, schools, small industries; the schools and the literacy campaigns change the outlook of the grasslands. Now 66 per cent of the nomad children go to school. They get favored treatment in the universities. An inverted quota system. And they intermarry.

Inner Mongolia is not just the scene of a social revolution in a nomad culture; it is the scene of a social revolution conditioned by national integration.

FROM LOYANG TO YENAN

Walking through the Loyang Tractor Works I fill a notebook with facts. The factory was constructed with technical assistance from the Soviet Union. The Soviet experts were withdrawn. It is now working below capacity level. Productivity is low. The percentage of unskilled workers is far too high. (Of a total labor force of "around" 20,000 in eight grades of skill, the average skill index should be 4.5 but is 2.2.) The quality of the tractors produced is bad. This leads to increased (unplanned) demand for spare parts. Thus agricultural production is upset as the tractors stand idle in the fields, and the production of the factory has to be switched over from complete tractors to spare parts. Workers are sent out together with the tractors to keep them running — a further drain on skilled manpower. Production is held up owing to lack of supplies. (Chung Lin-sheng, head of the general office in the works, complained that the special steel alloys are not forthcoming.)

This type of fact is important for the evaluation of Chinese industrial output. With minor variations (some factories were old and had been taken over from Chinese or foreign companies, some were recent and built entirely by Chinese technicians) the situation repeated itself in nearly every factory I saw. Low productivity. Mistakes in planning. Bottlenecks. Disorganization produced by the withdrawal of Soviet experts. (Leaving their half-finished jobs, taking their blueprints with them, and departing at a time when China already suffered from agricultural disasters and economic failures.) The enumeration of such facts makes the picture of Chinese development gloomy, full of disaster, nearly hopeless.

There is also another set of facts that can be noted down. The new canteens, the milk rations for workers, the medical care, the improved housing. Literacy courses, education for workers, the care for expectant mothers, social security. According to Asian standards, the social services are on a high level.

Twins, Loyang

(Left) Bicycle park outside Co-operative Department Store, Loyang; Old town, Loyang; Sunday morning, Loyang

Voluntary manual labor outside Loyang

Old men playing checkers

But there are also developments to be seen and foreseen that change the picture: innovations in technique raise productivity; unskilled workers in time become skilled workers; in China bad planning tends to correct itself by trial and error.

When all these facts and trends are complemented by a more general survey (population and birth/death rates, natural resources, educational system, transport network, capital investments, People's Commune organization, etc.), the result is presented as a true picture of Chinese development.

I hold that such facts and conclusions are vital for an understanding of what is happening. No analysis is possible without them. But a description on this level will not be sufficient. It is limited to purely technical, economic, and sociotechnological facts. This limitation to strange nonhuman truths is typical of our ("Western") culture at this stage of development. But it throws our picture of the reality of China (and other countries) out of focus.

The red tractors come off the assembly line. The drivers climb up. Slowly the tractors roll, one by one, out on the yard. These are not only tractors. They have become symbolic: tractors built despite difficulties and without foreign assistance.

Reckoned in purely economic terms, the Soviet withdrawal was negative. But in a wider human and cultural setting, this withdrawal became a boon in disguise. It made it possible for the regime — by still more strongly appealing to the national pride of the Chinese — to get support just because of the hardships.

The leaders in Peking have continually stressed the pride, the self-esteem of the Chinese people: poor but proud. A Chinese does not beg. We all share the hardships. Work is honorable. He who does not work, neither shall he eat. The ideas and ideals are egalitarian and puritanical. They are linked up both with the classical Chinese tradition and with the European (through Marx) tradition of puritanism, reformation, and revolution.

Model worker in front of wall newspaper, tractor works, Loyang

Tractor works, Loyang

Street library, children borrowing books, Sunday morning, Loyang

Old woman with bound feet making screen-blinds, home for the aged, Loyang

Woman worker, Loyang Tractor Works

Families visiting White Horse Temple, Loyang

When I believe that nothing can stop China from becoming one of the mightiest industrial powers within this generation, this belief is founded both on the economic and technical facts and on cultural and historical "nonweighable" facts. If I take the possibility of a third world war into account, the time scale will change. Industrialization will be delayed. But not much. And the trend will remain the same . . . if such a war would not lead to (the technically possible) mutual extermination — in which case the whole question is irrelevant.

There are economists who see the realities of a hungry and poor China making mistakes in planning, squandering her meager resources on reckless experiments, suffering from low productivity and overpopulation, and believe they have seen all the realities of China. But the three-day tourist going from Hong Kong to Canton and back and telling of a China without prostitutes, without graft, corruption, pickpockets, tipping, individual luxury, and flies has, in all his superficiality, grasped a more important reality.

The exhibition of Sian artists was like such exhibitions the world over. Most of what was shown was uninteresting. After all, the majority of artists, whether in China or Sweden, are of a leaden mediocrity. But there were some expressive woodcuts, some interesting traditional and semitraditional paintings, and a couple of oils in a heroic-naturalistic style that were notable. The workmanship and material technique were generally good, and even the gray majority of the exhibits had an aesthetic quality. That is high praise.

Afterwards we drank tea and talked. Suddenly, Li Tsai-shun from the Association of Art Workers in Sian turned to Gun and asked, "How do you keep contact with the masses in Sweden?"

"I am the masses," said Gun.

Nobody even smiled. Gun tried to explain that there was no such gap between artists and "ordinary" people in Sweden.

"We are artisans. That is all," she said.

I switched the conversation to the technique of oil painting.

Young intellectuals visiting
Lung-men National Monument, Loyang

Girl student, Lung-men, Loyang

Students, Sian University library

I know that it is nearly as impossible to make Chinese (or, in general, Asian) intellectuals understand the rather small difference between "scholars" and "people" in countries like the Scandinavian as for Scandinavians to understand what all this "remolding" and "meeting the masses" in China is about.

But this remolding of intellectuals in China is an attempt to overcome one of the serious handicaps of Asian cultures. (Gandhi made another attempt.) The abyss separating the learned man, the official or scholar, from the farmer, the laborer, is such that it makes nearly any social or economic development impossible. It has to be overcome.

I am not talking of the purely political "brainwashing" that prisoners of war, political prisoners, foreigners, and others have been subjected to. Not having experienced it, I have nothing new to say about it. The forcible re-education of enemies for political or propaganda purposes is neither new nor unusual. (In the words of Mencius one could say: "When one subdues men by force, they do not submit in their hearts. . . . When one subdues men by virtue, in their heart's core they are satisfied.")

When Gun said, "I am the masses," this was to the artists in Sian not only a joke in bad taste, it was also a preposterous lie; as she was an artist and as an artist is an intellectual, she could not by definition be one of the masses.

From what I have said, it is plain that I see the remolding as a necessity. A country like China, that stands before the choice of a rapid economic development or utter disaster, must achieve social and national integration to survive. This integration is in China brought about by implanting a new set of values among the former elite. (It needs to be pointed out that the guillotine, the firing squad, and the neck shot that have been the typical "Western" solutions to the question of former elites in a revolution are not the Chinese ones.)

Rehearsal of music students, Sian

That the remolding is painful is evident. But by linking up the new, socially useful values with selected ideas from the classical tradition, the Chinese leaders have given the remolded a firm moral framework to cling to. I am not sure that other basic readjustments, brought about elsewhere without such methods (the peasantry changed to big-city proletarians in the nineteenth century, the immigrants to America, the suburbanites of our welfare states today), were less painful. I would even say that the strong moral and puritanical tone in China alleviates the spiritual misery of uprooting and readjustment. This is not a popular thought to express. It runs counter to our (illusory) belief that our own adjustment is purely rational. I am also conscious of the possibility that I am rationalizing (in the Freudian sense) history, giving the flow of events a pattern to lighten the burden. As when Juvaini, the historian of the world conqueror Genghis Khan, writes about the Moslems slaughtered in the Mongol storm that, after all, they achieved martyrdom and thus reached paradise (which they otherwise would not have done).

For the young intellectuals brought up under Mao Tse-tung — and they already constitute nearly a majority — the problem is different. They are reacting to an established society. They adjust, not readjust. They do not carry a double set of values. (The situation might be better understood by looking at first- and second-generation immigrants to America.)

It is sometimes said that "Chinese culture" will be destroyed with the remolding of the old intellectuals. But cultures are durable. In fact, remolding has not succeeded in changing some of the fundamental attitudes of Chinese intellectuals. Among them the deep conviction that they are called upon to lead the people.

This might be most easily seen in the discussions going on about literature, opera, and art. To meet the masses is a difficult undertaking. Especially as the masses are vulgar: village, villager, villain. I have a strong suspicion — after reading their articles — that the old Chinese intellectuals that have been remolded have never met the masses; they have met the idealized masses: a devulgarized vulgus.

Studying Peking opera, Sian

Students, Sian University

Girl studying music, Sian

Rehearsing ballet, Sian

It is not the people — the peasants (a village that has had a group of old intellectuals for remolding is then exempt from this duty for some years), the workers, the "common men" — that demand the "cleansing" of the folk tales, shadow plays, and operas from sexual coarseness, ghosts, feudal characters, to change them to purifying tales about People's Liberation Army heroes. Neither is it the old actors. I doubt whether it even is Mao Tse-tung (though quotations of his are used in the process); his poem "The Immortals," for instance, would surely be branded as rightist and feudal if written by someone else. With reason the moral fury of neophytes has always been feared.

The integration process is ambiguous and — to speak in European associations — the social morality of the old intellectuals often seems to turn from Thomas Münzer to Girolamo Savonarola.

It happened in Sian. It had happened in Silinhot and Loyang. It was to happen in Tali and Mangshih. On Saturday evening the kanpus came to town from all the countryside. They gathered at the guest house. Leaning out through my window, I could hear the echoes of expectant laughter. Young girls in black trousers and cotton blouses holding each other around the waist. Made up with lipstick, having pink ribbons in their hair. Giggling.

The young kanpus of China dance every Saturday night. All over the country, from Inner Mongolia to Yunnan, the dance bands strike up as the sun is setting. Young kanpus dancing under the garlanded portrait of Chairman Mao. On a hot night in Sian listening to the dance band, I nearly had fallen asleep when I suddenly become wide awake realizing that my prejudices were showing. I had not found the dance noteworthy. But my lack of interest in the dance was as symptomatic as the dance itself. I had only registered: "Saturday evening dance."

But in Chinese reality these dances are a complete break with tradition and old-type official behavior. It is a break, but not a spontaneous one. It is a carefully organized break. With traditions from the Yenan days. To the young and adjusted are given both the liberty of falling in love and the careers open to talent. In the long run, that is of greater importance than the remolding of old scholars.

Lovers, Sian;

Tea shop, Sian

Peasant leaders of Wang Mang village

Peasant washing in irrigation canal,
Wang Mang village, Honan

78

Intellectuals visiting Wang Mang village

When I was fifteen I heard of the Long March. That was during World War II. And even though we have had the misfortune to be born in an age of great historical interest when there are wars and adventures enough, the story of the Long March and the Caves of Yenan to me then assumed nearly epical proportions. Now, twenty years later I stood in an earthen cave in Yenan looking at a small zinc bathtub.

"That was the tub that Chairman Mao used."

The young guide pointed at the object. His voice was reverent. Looking at this hallowed tub, I felt ill at ease. As if the epos had ended with a slightly obscene pun. ("Every tub on its own bottom," my English language teacher had used to say.)

But Yenan was not the final chapter. And Mao Tse-tung has never revisited his legendary guerilla capital among the loessial hills since he retreated from it in 1947 for the final struggle that would carry him to the proclamation of the Chinese People's Republic from the Gate of Heavenly Peace in Peking on October 1, 1949 (that gate, then decayed, later restored, from which the imperial edicts had been given the kneeling officials during the time of the empire of all under heaven). History is no epos.

But the epos has a function in society. And the story of Mao Tse-tung, the Long March, and the Caves of Yenan now fills the role of the founding myth of People's China. Though the myth is factual.

Viewing this story as an epos, one can say that the tub expresses one stage in the story of the hero. (That Mao of whom Edgar Snow wrote, ". . . 'Ma-ti, t'ai jeh-ti — Rape it, it's hot,' said Mao, taking off his pants and sitting down again as naturally as Gandhi in his loincloth.") That was the folk hero during a pause in the battles. Battles of which he himself made poems. (As the hero in the ancient epos stepped outside himself to sing his battle.)

Keen is the west wind;
In the endless void the wild geese cry at the frosty morning moon.
The frosty morning moon.
The clatter of horses' hoofs rings sharp,
And the bugle's note is muted. . . .
The sky is high, the clouds are pale.
We watch the wild geese flying south till they vanish;
If we reach not the Great Wall, we are not true men!
Already we have come ten thousand leagues.
High on the crest of Liupan Mountain
Our banners idly wave in the west wind. . . .

And even the stage on which the hero performed is classical. The military reason why the Red Army on its Long March battled its way to the poor loessial hills of North Shensi had been stated more than two thousand years ago by the historian (read by Mao, the student) Ssu-ma Ch'ien: "The Ts'in country, inside the passes, is a state predestined for victory by the lay of its land alone; access to it rendered difficult because of the belt formed around it by the river and the mountains, it is suspended a thousand li above the rest of the empire. With but twenty thousand men, it can hold off one million men armed with lances."

Had Mao Tse-tung died during the war and been buried in Yenan, he would have been one of the heroes of Chinese history. (Of this he himself was conscious. Which, I believe, explains the strange tone of understanding detachment with which in his poems he speaks of the long-dead emperors.) But he fulfilled the epical story and could decree the new, unified Chinese state — the first Han state of China having real control of China's territory since the fall of the Ming Dynasty — from the Imperial City.

And the grave of the Yellow Emperor at Hwangling was once more restored, as it had been restored by the first Ming emperor after the Mongols were driven out nearly five hundred years before.

River crossings on the road towards Hwangling and Yenan

River crossings on the road towards Hwangling and Yenan

Rain in Hwangling (Slogans painted on wall read:
"Going all out!"
"Aiming high and achieving greater, faster, better, and more
economical results in building socialism!")

But, as Mao himself pointed out, victory was in itself but the first step in a ten-thousand-li march. The epos now was to give inspiration and ideals during this new long march of "maybe five generations." And the road to economic development and a better life is a hard one, a dusty road — gray without glamour.

The man Mao Tse-tung becomes hidden behind the mythical hero. The heroics were real, but they already become transformed by legend.

"Here Chairman Mao sat writing during the bombardment," the young guide said.

The room was bare, just a wooden table and a chair. The walls were of mud bricks; the roof was thin.

"And the bombs were falling. And the other leading comrades pleaded with Chairman Mao to go to the bomb shelter. But Chairman Mao just said, 'Don't disturb me. Bombs are not dangerous. I'm writing.' He was very brave."

Wang stood beside me. An old Communist limping from a wound in 1940. ("I was a student. Took part in the demonstrations after the killings in Shanghai, 1935. Then I was a school-teacher. When the Japanese came, I became a guerilla, later a Communist, a guerilla leader. So thus I worked politically with gun in my hand for fifteen years.") The guide seemed to irritate him. He interrupted the guide and we left.

"Chairman Mao," said Wang, "is a good military man. Not a man of sham heroics."

Thinking about the young guide and his story, I realized that his legend of the brave Chairman Mao during the bombardment of Yenan had stepped out of an oil painting. Chairman Mao in his room during the bombardment. Flashes seen through the open window. Maps on the wall. Brush in hand. Sitting at the table. His left leg stretched. Trousers with mended knees. Peasant footwear. Far-seeing eyes. Don't disturb me. I write the future. A gesture of the hand holding the brush indicating this.

The bell at the Yenan pagoda

Women washing clothes, Yen River, Yenan

In terms more acceptable to the Chinese today, I could say that the experiences of the Revolution and the Yenan time must be used to instill "the Yenan style — hard work and plain living" in the new generations. (Maybe five generations.) So that they don't grow soft and complacent and give up the fundamental ideas.

A week later, just as Wang was leaving for Peking and Gun and I were to move to the village, we all sat drinking hot wine in the Yenan guest house taking leave.

Suddenly Wang looked at me and said, "My eldest boy is fourteen years old. He goes to school. One day when I came home I saw that his neck was dirty. It was black with grime. I asked him why. He answered: 'In our school we pupils have decided to live in the Yenan style.' I had to explain to him that being a revolutionary is not the same as no longer washing your neck."

Earlier that day we had visited the Cave of Ten Thousand Buddhas, once the headquarters of the Yenan press office, now just a national monument. I thought about the description of Yenan in the *Concise Geography of China:* "Heart of the revolution . . . attracts many visitors and tourists. Places of interest include . . . the rows upon rows of caves, many of which served as dwellings of the leaders of the party . . ." Now Mao Tse-tung and his generation are ascending to the pantheon of Chinese history in a mist of legends.

For the generations taking over, the "thought of Chairman Mao" is to remain as an inspiration. But the old men now dying — the real men, not the legendary ones – – worry. The road is so long.

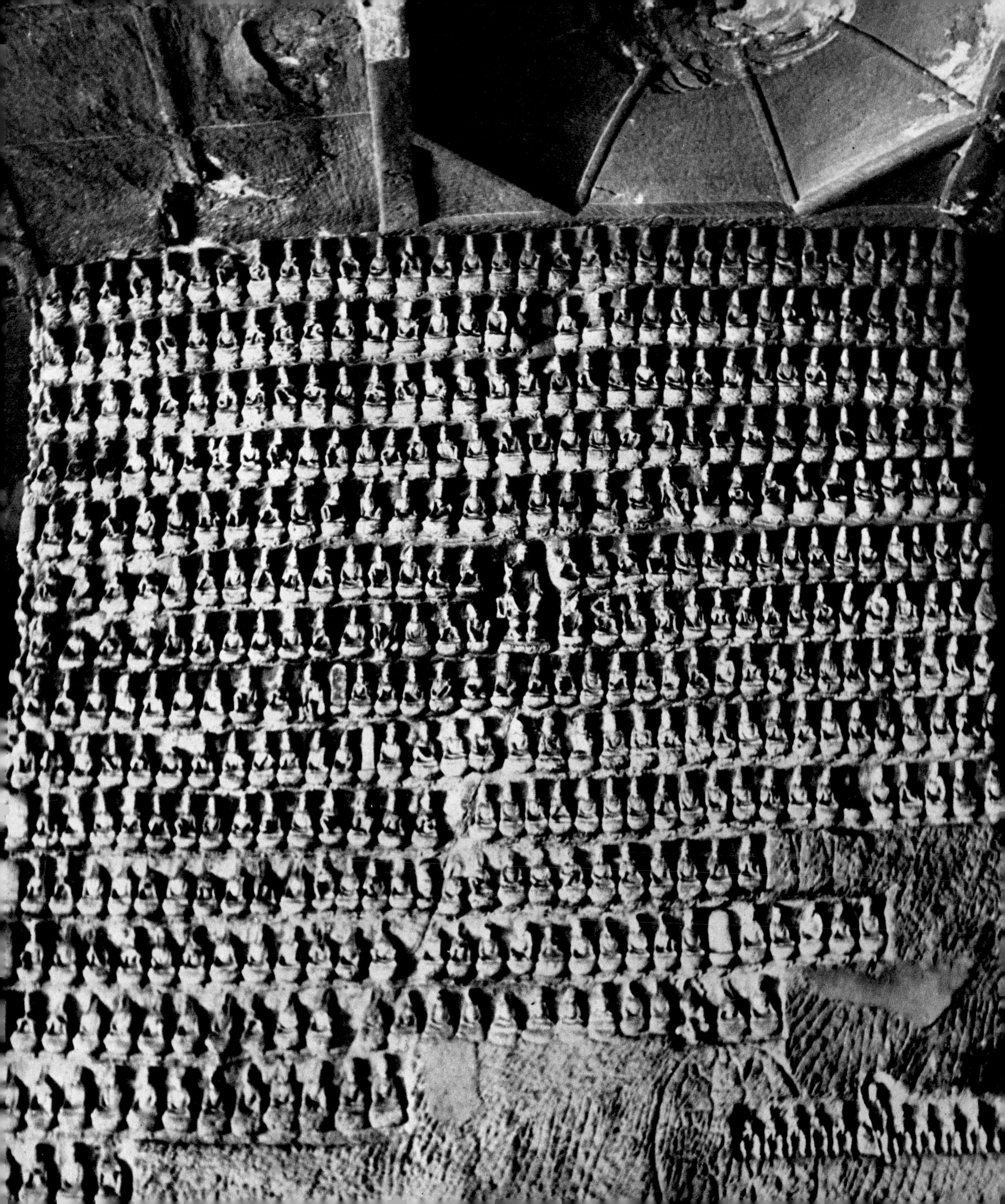

Pottery works, Yenan

(Overleaf) Yenan

Liu Ling Village in North Shensi

But, to move from myth to reality, Liu Ling is a small village. Fifty families live here in caves dug out of the yellow loess. However, this sentence is equivocal. "Caves" is a loaded word. It would be wrong to call the villagers of North Shensi troglodytes. In dry loessial earth, caves are not bad dwellings; they are rational — cool in summer, warm in winter. Such caves do not take less manpower to build than houses.

We spent a month in this village, trying to achieve a description of peasant reality. My diary for September 4 says:

Sitting outside the cave. Late evening. Sun already hidden behind the hills. Listen to the news broadcast from BBC on my transistor radio. Switching it off, I hear the night watchman in the melon fields playing. (Against foxes, it is said. What foxes? Living, "real" foxes or spirit foxes?) Calm. Evening smell. Ochre hills. Burning, reddening, darkening (umber). Violet haze. Night. Fu Hai-tsao's dog barks twice. Quiet.

This description of shapes and colors seen, sounds heard, odors (human excrement and undefinable scent of earth, vegetation, night) smelled is a true description. But it conveys nothing of the village.

The legends about the Revolution do not change the fact that there has been a revolution. The peasants of China had been marching. As in all of Asia, the village was to give the key to the understanding of what happened — and why. So I left my private impressions for what they were worth and listened to the villagers when they told of their lives. Fu Hai-tsao, thirty-nine years old, spoke of his childhood:

"We came to Yenan from Hengshan when I was five. That was during the great famine of 1928. We had been thrown out. My father brought the family with him here. Father starved to death the next year. We went about begging in 1929. We had nothing to eat. Father went to Chaochuan to gather firewood and beg food, but he didn't get any. He was carrying elm leaves and firewood when he fell by the roadside. We waited for him all night. In the morning, when

he hadn't come, Mother said, 'Now, let's go and see what's happened to him.' Then Mother and Uncle and I walked along the road to Chaochuan. I was the one who saw him first. He was lying on his face and was dead. The elm leaves and firewood were still there. The elm leaves were for us to eat.

"He wasn't ill; he had just starved to death. Mother says he used to be big and strong and had been a good worker, thoughtful and kind to the family and open-handed if anyone was ill. That is my earliest memory: of always being hungry, and Father lying there dead in the road."

Another voice, that of Ching Chung-ying, fifty-four years old:

"When I was twenty, the great famine came. That was in 1928. One of my brothers died. After that Father and I and my three other brothers went to Shansi. It was better there. We sold my two youngest brothers. We were forced to do that in order to survive. We got twenty-eight silver dollars for one and twenty silver dollars for the other. I don't know where they went. I have never heard of them since. After that it was only Father and I and my younger brother, Ching Chung-wan. He also lives in Liu Ling now. I fell ill. But I survived and two years later we came back to Hengshan again."

And a woman, Tu Fang-lan, fifty-six years old:

"My parents-in-law died in 1929. Later, we went to Paoan to take service with a landlord. But my husband died five days after we got there. Our eldest son was then thirteen and our second eight. We had of course nowhere to go, so we stayed there in Paoan, and the two elder boys began working as herdsmen in order to help support the family. I worked in the fields and life was very hard for us. The rich had all the food they wanted. They ate their fill of wheat. But we had nothing. We were poor. I went hungry to such an extent that my hair fell out in great tufts if I pulled at it. That time in Paoan was the worst I experienced. If second brother had not helped me with a little rice, we would have starved to death." She wept as she talked.

When I published these stories, I found that many readers refused to believe them. I suspect that this refusal is not only stupidity but also fear. A child's image of a world of "schemes" and

101

"evil plotters" seems to many safer than a world of poverty and misery and starvation and peasant war. But even if it hurts their illusions, these yellow loess gorges ("Ochre hills. Burning, reddening, darkening . . .") had been the setting for human suffering and peasant misery also according to informants other than the peasants themselves.

"On sale at the principal offices of Thos. Cook & Son" in the years just before World War I was a *Handbook for China* by Carl Crow:

> *Shensi province: The province suffered severely during the Mohammedan rebellion of 1874, which is estimated to have swept away about half the population. . . . One of the worst famines in the recent history of China was that in Shensi which followed soon after the Boxer uprising. In some districts the death rate was 70 per cent . . . the deaths were about $2\frac{1}{2}$ million.*

And O. Edmund Clubb, the former U.S. Consul General in Peiping, writes in *Twentieth-Century China,* 1964:

> *A Nanking official was quoted in January, 1931, as stating that two million persons had died of famine in Shensi province alone in the past few years, with thousands of villages become desolate and with four hundred thousand persons sold into slavery.*

That there sprang rebellion and peasant war out of this misery was quite according to the traditions of Chinese history. Take the fall of the Ch'in Dynasty in 209 B.C. as recorded by the grand historian of China, Ssu-ma Ch'ien, *c.* 145–90 B.C. (transl. Burton Watson, New York, 1961):

> *Yet Ch'en She, born in a humble hut with tiny windows and a wattle door, a day laborer in the fields and a garrison conscript, whose abilities would not match even the average . . . stepped from the ranks of the common soldiers, rose up from the paths of the fields, and led a band of some hundred poor weary soldiers in revolt against Ch'in. They cut down trees to make their weapons and raised their flags on garden poles, and the whole world gathered like a cloud . . .*

When Pai Yu-teh, a veteran kanpu of sixty, talks of the Revolution, it is a peasant war that he describes:

"In 1931, 1932, and 1933, I kept hearing about Liu Chih-tan and how there were revolutionaries in Suiteh and Tzechang who had destroyed the landowners and done away with taxes. That made a deep impression on me. . . . In 1935, Liu Chih-tan was operating in Nanliang and in Wuchi. There was a lot of talk then about the Red Army. In April that year Liu Chih-tan sent a guerilla group to Thirty-Mile Village to wipe out an armed landowner group. The Red Army's slogan was: 'Down with the local landowners! Down with the local despots! Down with imperialism! Divide the land equally! Free the women! Abolish taxes!' Thirty-Mile Village was not far away, of course, and I talked about what had happened with my best friend, Han Pei-hsin. He and I worked together, and we had already been profoundly impressed by what we had heard of the happenings in Suiteh and Tzechang. Now, we told each other that we ought to go across the hills and see what they were doing in Thirty-Mile Village. After all, we wanted everyone to be equal and all landowners and bureaucrats to be destroyed. So, one night, Han Pei-hsin and I set out across the mountain to see if we could find the Red Army. It was chilly and we had only one quilted coat between us, and that was seven years old. Han Pei-hsin later become party secretary in a liberated *hsien* [administrative unit, roughly equivalent to a county] and died in 1942 of tuberculosis and undernourishment. . . . It was now my job to organize the people of the neighboring villages."

The peasant war was not a simple affair of all peasants suddenly making revolt. Ma Chen-hai, sixty-five years old, said:

"I remember the day the Red Guard reached the village. That was in November, 1934. People were saying, 'There are Red Guard men in the village.' We were all afraid. I scarcely dared to go out. If I did go out and met one of my neighbors, we spoke softly together. One of the neighbors I met on the road said to me in a whisper, 'They're saying we shan't be oppressed any more.' It was only propagandists from the Red Guard that had come to the village, not the soldiers of the army.

Li Yiu-hua, the Old Secretary

Li Shang-wa
(Below) Kao Pin-ying; Wife of
Ching Chung-ying with grandchildren

"The propagandist who came then was Kao Wen-shen. He was a man with a swarthy, sun-burned face. He was a poor farmer from a neighboring village and I knew him. No, I don't know how he got into the Red Army or how he became a propagandist. But now I heard that he was in the village and was talking about the revolution. He stayed one night with us, and then he went on somewhere else. Some days later, we heard that he had been executed by the Kuomintang. He had come to another village and one of the poor farmers with whom he talked informed his landlord about him and the landlord had sent for the Kuomintang, and they had come in the night and shot him on the spot. . . . Then suddenly all these propagandists vanished. The Red Guard never came and the Kuomintang were still there and everything was the same as before."

Battles were fought, trees were cut down to make spears, flags were fluttering from garden poles — the "old hundred names" of China were in rebellion. The high and mighty were brought down. Mau Ke-yeh, fifty-nine years old, said:

"We had only twenty Red Army men, but the Self-Defense Corps from all the villages had come too. The landowner's house was now surrounded by hundreds of men. We set up red flags on all the hills round about, and there were lots of them, so the horizon was quite red all around Ma Sho-yen. Then we all called to the landowner and held up our spears and said, 'If you don't give us your land and if you don't give us your rifles, you won't survive. You will die tonight.' After a while he came out. He was a big man in his fifties with a mustache, and he said, 'As long as I can keep my life, the land and rifles don't matter.' When we had got the rifles, we let him go and he ran away to Kanchuan, where he had relatives. No one was even wounded in that action. And as soon as the landowner had fled, the villagers emerged; you see, they had been forced to stay with the landowner because they had been afraid he would report them as 'bandits' or 'Red Army men,' and he had told them that if he did that, the Kuomintang would cut off their heads. They were all glad now, and we held a big meeting and divided up the land and all the landowner's possessions."

When we were staying in Liu Ling village and I was recording the stories of the peasants, I read *Water Margin,* the classical Chinese novel of the robbers of Liang Shan Po. The night after I had taken down Mau Ke-yeh's story, I noted in my diary: *"Water Margin,* p. 904" The quotation was:

Shih Chin took the men to the house of the woman Li Shui-lan and killed everybody there. Sung Chiang distributed all the goods in the prefect's house among the people. He also issued a proclamation: "We have killed the officials who injured you people, so that now you may continue your avocations without fear."

Chiang Kai-shek and his followers called the rebelling peasants "bandits." To a certain extent that is correct. If banditry is seen as a social phenomenon, it is a prepolitical social movement. But as banditry seldom is used in that particular sense, the words "Red bandits" cloud the issue.

To this North Shensi of peasant war, where the slogans and ideas were more chiliastic than political ("We had meetings at which we talked of how all humanity was to be freed of all oppression and all misfortune and need, and how all people were to become brothers and live as equals all over the world." Li Yiu-hua on the North Shensi Soviet Region.), came Mao Tse-tung. Here in this intersection between peasant reality and the "legend," something radically new was born. When Mao came, the peasant rebellion was changed to a political war that was to be of worldwide importance.

Mao Tse-tung had then been an outlaw, marching with gun in hand for eight years. He had led uprisings. Been defeated. Led new uprisings. Seen most of his followers sacrificed. He had been looked on askance by his own party until, in the middle of defeat, he had won the party. His ideas had developed and changed during these years. Now, from these poor loess hills he was to start out on a new type of war. Not a peasant war any longer, not only a national war, not a class war in the orthodox Communist sense but a new type of war that was to unite these elements until the whole of China was taken over — and changed.

Teacher Kou giving pupils boiling water for refreshment during break

Li Kuei-ying making noodles for festival

Pai Yu-teh said: "Chairman Mao came to us and spoke of the necessity for forming a united front [against Japan]. The Central Committee now stopped our activities against the landowners. They insisted that we had been guilty of departing from the correct revolutionary way, so we reinvestigated the true class circumstances of every family. We had been far too strict, we were told. We were now to fight shoulder-to-shoulder even with landlords." Pai Yu-teh himself was given the word to prepare for co-operation with the Kuomintang troops: "Their fighting morale was poor, of course, they had no food, they were hungry and cold, and lost all the engagements they were in with us, for they were fighting far from their homes in a war they did not understand. The first conferences between us and the Northeastern Army took place in Tungchwankou, about twenty li from Yenan. . . . We sat in a stone cave and had a friendly chat. That was the first step in our collaboration that finally led to Chiang Kai-shek's being taken prisoner in Sian and compelled to go to war with Japan."

The slogans "Chinese do not fight Chinese!" and "Unite against the Japanese invaders!" could of course also be experienced in a different fashion by those who became victims of this unity. Li Yiu-hua spoke of the fate of his village, where they had made a revolt in order that all men become brothers:

"Right up to the end of May, 1937, when the enemy attacked us from Hengshan, we had no idea that they were going to launch an attack. . . . Our guerillas were retreating the whole time. We never saw the Red Army. When we farmers saw the enemy's troops coming, we said: 'We are helpless. There's nothing we can do.' We could not even defend ourselves; when the enemy rounded us up to build forts for them . . . we kept asking each other, 'When will our government come back? When will our Red Army come? If only we could hear from them, and if only we knew where they were now, so we could work for them.' But however much we asked, nobody knew where our government had gone or where the Red Army was, and we never heard from the party and just wondered."

110

The little Liu boy

Children sleeping and eating

113

The ability to retreat is a necessary virtue for the man leading a war or a revolution. To sacrifice poor friends to placate mighty enemies thus is an obvious need for the successful revolutionary. Mao did not gladly — cynically — sacrifice Li Yiu-hua and his fellow villagers. But he did it. The peasant war was transformed into a national war. What is unique is not that Mao unleashed and led a peasant war or that Mao was prepared to sacrifice his followers for what he considered the higher interests of the nation, but that he managed to infuse that spirit among his peasant followers. He is not only the representative of a new type of guerilla warfare but of a new type of peasant war.

Pai Yu-teh said: "One night in May, 1936, the Peace-Conserving Brigade came to our United Front Bureau in the Date Garden. They were under the command of Li Han-hua and, in breach of agreement, they were armed. I wasn't in the office at the time, but they took four others prisoner: Li San-chi, Ma Chan-piao, Liu Chung-piao, and a comrade called Han, but I have forgotten the rest of his name. These four were responsible for the work of the United Front in the Date Garden open market. But they were irresponsibly credulous and not sufficiently prepared for the class hatred of the landowners, so they were all captured together and had their heads cut off that same night.

"The difficult thing here was that the pact between the Northeastern Army and us was secret. We discussed the matter with the Northeastern Army and it was all hushed up. Of course we would have liked to avenge our comrades, but for political reasons we had to pretend that nothing had happened. The important thing was to preserve the United Front. That sort of thing happened quite frequently. I cannot remember the event ever being taken up afterwards, and no plaque was ever put up in their memory."

The villagers gave Mao the force necessary for the revolution, the war, the victory. Now they are to give the means for converting China into a major industrial world power.

Village latrines

115

Chia Fu-lan at the mill; Li Hai-yuan at the mill

Carrying the melons up the village street; Manure loaded on donkeys to be carried up the hillside to the fields

"The years pass," said Tung Yang-chen, thirty-five years old. "They are all one like another. We begin with the spring plowing and continue with it for a month. We sow millet, then kaoliang and maize. We plow for two different kinds of 'sticky millet' — that takes ten days; then we sow. We turn the soil and sow buckwheat. Then we begin weeding the fields, and we keep on with that the whole time till we harvest, one field after the other, and then begin again with the first field. We harvest the wheat and bring it down off the hillside. We begin threshing the wheat and plowing up the wheat fields. We sow wheat and harvest buckwheat and then the two kinds of 'sticky millet,' millet, maize, and beans. We bring our harvest down off the hillside with carrying poles. We thresh and we finish threshing towards the end of the year. In January we have winter, and then we rest and gather fuel and that sort of thing, unless there's some water-regulating work or something else on the go, and after that we begin the year with plowing again."

As the years, so the days. Ma Hung-tsai's wife was twenty-five years old. She said: "My husband goes out to the fields at daybreak. When he has gone, I make breakfast for myself and the children and for him. A special food carrier from his group fetches him breakfast. He is plowing today. There is a lot to do now, but in the winter he usually stays at home till he has had breakfast, about seven o'clock.

"I myself usually go out to work at about seven or eight o'clock. I get home to the cave about twelve and make dinner. My husband rests while I am preparing the food; then we eat and he has a little sleep. Sometimes he helps me. He looks after the children. We do help each other at times. We are a young couple, of course. At two in the afternoon, we go out to work again, and we usually get home about eight in the evening. Then we have supper and go to bed."

Work is hard. Food is millet porridge. "That's filling," as Li Yiu-hua said. "Wheat is more of a luxury. There's no strength in it."

Chang Chu-liang; Pupils,
Liu Ling village school

It was raining and the cave was cold. I was alone. We were taking a ten-minute break. I wasn't feeling very well. My liver had been giving me trouble again this past week. Old Doctor Kao had examined me last night. Felt my pulse and said, "Too much cold and wind." Which summed up the sensation quite accurately. He had given me a herbal medicine to drink.

I had just finished an interview with an old woman, Chia Ying-lan. She was fifty-three years of age; in Sweden she would have been middle-aged. But in the Sweden of fifty years ago she would have been what she was here, an old woman. It had been a painful interview. She had been crying. And I had had to ask questions, each more personal than the one before. The talk had taken a long time. During most of it she had been weeping. And I had felt like a heel. Just sitting there, foreign and cold, and interrupting her tears, "And then what happened?"

The last thing she said (turning around in the doorway looking at me) was, "I have never even told my son all this."

Afterwards I looked over my notes of what the women gossiped about her and her son. She can't find a wife for him. "In all probability he will remain unmarried and that worries Chia Ying-lan greatly, because then the family will die out."

I wondered about my work and what I was trying to do in this village. It is both fascinating and interesting to try to see the pattern of social development. I wanted to try to make a report on a Chinese village — let the individuals speak for themselves. But even by asking I was causing pain.

Now, when going through my notes from the Chinese journeys, I feel that I commit a double treason. By placing all these individuals inside a pattern that I shape (even if I believe it to be consistent with reality) I am once more muting them, deindividualizing them. But there is no other way to form a pattern than by selection. Though I had to drive Chia Ying-lan, a woman who had experienced much suffering, to weep through a whole day to reach it. Both that day in the cave in Liu Ling and today in Sweden I sense the vileness of the writer's role.

Old Doctor Kao

119

While I was working in Liu Ling it struck me that many of the arguments about development and ideals that the politically responsible peasants used were very similar to those used in the "welfare states." Lo Han-hong, the young bookkeeper, said:

"People live better than they used to, and they are beginning to have new needs. This began immediately after the East Shines Red Higher Agricultural Co-operative was formed, by people starting to whitewash the caves and get decorations for them. What's happened now is that people are providing themselves with means of transport. Almost every household has already got itself a two-wheeled cart on rubber wheels. These can either be pulled or harnessed to a bicycle. Some have also begun getting bicycles. There are more and more bicycles all the time. And those who have carts and bicycles are now wanting to have radios and alarm clocks. There is no limit to their needs. The better life is, the greater become one's requirements."

Speaking about social care of the aged and ill, the leader of the Liu Ling Brigade, Feng Chang-yeh, said:

"At the same time, we have to see that the social grants don't become so big that social help is greater than the workers' incomes. One must not undermine the value of work. But one has to see that everyone, even those who for various reasons have got into difficulties, has the chance to live a decent life. You will understand that better if you will take a look at the figures. The year before the formation of the Liu Ling People's Commune, 1957, we in the East Shines Red Higher Agricultural Co-operative handed over as social help 3,360 *jin* of corn and 6,000 *jin* of fuel. During 1958, when Liu Ling People's Commune was formed, these figures rose to 13,900 and 14,000, respectively, and in 1959, the first whole year with the commune, when we had stabilized the position, 13,300 and 16,000; and last year, 1961, we had got up to 16,300 and 18,000.

"There you have the development. I consider this one of the most important changes of recent years. Illness, death, and accident are no longer catastrophes. Citizens now have security."

Plow and harrow

These statements — that life is getting better, "The better life is, the greater become one's requirements," "Citizens now have security" — ought, I believe, to be taken at face value. The basis for this belief is to be found in my book *Report from a Chinese Village* (1964). But — and this is also important — Chinese society today is not that society of "brotherhood" of which the original peasant revolutionaries talked. I would even go so far as to say that Lo Han-hong's ideal of a future society is close to that of a good and law-abiding citizen of one of the welfare states. The ideals of the original revolutionaries might already be as far from the present society as those of Thomas Paine are from the U.S.A., and the "République des Égaux" of Babeuf is from present-day France.

But the Chinese village is, of course, not a society in which a Swedish farmer would find either a minimum level of prosperity and social security or response for his social ideas. That ought to be self-evident. It is not. I have been asked by serious students of sociology, eager for knowledge, how come the Chinese don't understand that machines are more rational and economical than raw manpower. They had never even thought about the real difficulty of developing a country without capital. A country where the dividing line between production and consumption is so thin that a fortnight without rain can wipe it out.

The political and economic motive behind the drive for collectivization and People's Communes is simple to understand. The only real resource of China is manpower. Traditionally, winter is a slack season. The peasants have rested (hungrily) on their kangs. Organization was to be a substitute for capital. If 200,000,000 men were utilized 10 hours a day for 30 days, they would yield 60,000,000,000 work hours. That was capital. That much of this organization breaks down, that much is badly planned should not hide the truth that this was their only way. From where else would they get capital? The freedom of choice for China's political leaders was severely limited.

(Overleaf) Plowing;
Li Yiu-hua

YUNNAN AND THE BURMA ROAD

We came to Kunming in December. The weather was beautiful. An everlasting spring. Peking had been cold and dusty. I had felt as if all of Gobi were settling on my skin. (But it was better now than formerly, the Chinese said. They had planted 30,000,000 trees around Peking to bind the dust.) There had been big demonstrations passing outside my window as I sat writing on Liu Ling. I listened to the radio. I read Klaus Mehnert's *Peking and Moscow*. On the flyleaf I had written: "This day, as I read the experts, is the fourth day of the demonstration. 1,200,000 Chinese have marched past my windows. If the experts thought of the poverty of peasants in this world and read their Bible more carefully, they would understand better. Jeremiah 8:10–12 says more about the Chinese feeling for the Soviet leaders than any expert I have read."

Now we had come to this beautiful spring weather. And I just kept on thinking of the Liu Ling village. The draft was finished and sent to Stockholm. I wondered about my own conclusions.

Liu Ling had been a microcosm of China. It had functioned by social control and social morality. During the whole development of the co-operatives, interminable discussions, urged on carefully by the party, had marked every step. Until the People's Commune. Then it had seemingly been a *pro forma* discussion. "In 1958 there was a new thing," Tung Yang-chen had said. "People were talking then about a people's commune. I decided then, at the very beginning, that I would first hear what the party said and follow it and not argue. Because the party had always been right before." I could not judge whether the discussion that had been going on for twenty-five years in Liu Ling was now slowly ebbing out.

The birth-control campaign, on the other hand, was lively in Liu Ling — though not yet in the whole country. Li Kuei-ying had explained how they convinced husbands: "The whole thing is voluntary. . . . In certain families with lots of children the women would like birth control, but their husbands won't let them. In those families the husbands say, 'There's not going to be any family planning here!' Then we women go and try to talk sense into them."

*Main street, Kunming,
permanent stand for demonstrations*

And this talking of sense is in China talking of virtue. A new type of virtue, though — social and not familial. "We say, 'Look how many children you have. Your wife looks after the household and sees to all the children and she makes shoes and clothes for both of you and the children, but you don't think of all she has to do or of her health but just make her with child again and again. Wait now for three or four years. Then you can have more if you want.' Usually, they will eventually say, 'If it isn't to go on all one's life, then all right.' But in other cases, the husband just says, 'No.' Then we women speak to him about it every day, till he agrees to birth control. No husband has yet managed to stand out for any length of time when we are talking to him." And then comes the operational sentence: "Actually, of course, they know that we are right. They know, of course, that they are responsible. It's only their pride that stands in the way, and we have to tell them that such pride is false and not all right." By reason virtue shall triumph! But . . .

Looking over my material, there was also another tendency. The standards were rising. Slowly. The surplus was being converted into capital investments. It was considered amoral (because it hindered capital formation) to want personal privileges or property. But when Lo Han-hong told of the big discussion that had led to the decision to buy an electric pump, he said, "After that everyone was agreed, and the proposal was accepted and all the representatives were happy. At the end of the meeting we all forgathered and ate wheat noodles." I asked him, "Who paid for the noodles?" After a moment, he answered, "The noodles were paid for by the welfare fund. This decision that we should eat at the welfare fund's expense was taken last thing at the representatives' meeting.") And when I checked with Liu Hsin-min, the party secretary of the Liu Ling People's Commune, about what had been the result of the co-operation inside the commune (which was one of the main ideas of the commune principle), he said:

Tien Chih lake, Kunming, Yunnan

Street scenes, Kunming

Children window-shopping, Kunming; Children playing war, Kunming

"In the winter of 1959–60 Liu Ling Labor Brigade carried out a very big water-regulation project. This cost a total of 14,772 days' work of which Liu Ling Labor Brigade itself contributed only 4,172. Liu Ling Brigade first repaid a total of 1,568 days' work to the other two brigades which had collaborated, Chungchuan Labor Brigade and The Sun Rises Labor Brigade. They got roughly 800 days' work each. After that, however, it become difficult to repay in work and, after lengthy meetings and much discussion, we agreed that Liu Ling Labor Brigade could pay in cash. Negotiations took a long time. In the end the parties agreed that payment should be at 0.80 yuan per day's work performed. That was roughly 0.30 yuan below the current valuation of a day's work. It was a matter of 8,532 days' work. Since then no labor exchange project of this magnitude has been carried out between brigades."

I knew how the peasants of Liu Ling struggled to get a better life. And I understood why they had driven this hard bargain with their neighbors. But it had upset the main idea of the people's commune: to organize for better utilization of manpower.

In Kunming I continued asking about corruption, misappropriation of funds, and embezzlement. In Lung Chen People's Commune outside Kunming, I spoke with the director, Kao Yung-ching. (His hands, I noted, were those of an intellectual. He was not using them for manual labor.)

"There is embezzlement. Some days ago a team leader was found out. He had stolen three hundred yuan from his team. He was criticized. Made self-criticism. Promised never to steal any more. Expelled from the party. Has to pay it all back."

They didn't go to court. They arranged everything inside the village. That was according to Chinese tradition as well as to Mao's rationality. "The Soviets," a Chinese said, "shot too many people. You don't cure corruption that way. Then nobody wants to correct the neighbor who is stealing the common funds. Violence ought to be used sparingly."

I wondered. What happens if morality breaks under the pressure of poverty?

(From top to bottom)
Drying chili, Tali
Freshening vegetables in water for market, Tali
Fishing, Tali

Going west on the Burma Road is a beautiful journey. But it is also an exercise in switching historical reference points. According to the dictionary, the Burma Road was built in A.D. 1937–39. That is very true. Also rather nonsensical. The road follows one of the old silk roads through Asia; and ever since the reign of Emperor Wu Ti of the Han Dynasty (140–87 B.C.) it has played a part in the foreign policy of the Chinese state.

The motor road was, of course, built nearly thirty years ago; it has now been asphalted and widened, and is heavily traveled. The road — like every such road — is of military importance. But the main importance today, as formerly, is for trade. Two years earlier, Gun and I had been traveling in northern Burma during the Kachin rebellion. When we stayed at the Bhamo guest house, we saw trucks pass to the east.

We asked the district collector, "What are those?"

"Oh, just smugglers."

"Smugglers?"

"Yes, they take care of the trade with China."

Since then the border trade has been regularized. Oil and gasoline, machinery and spare parts come up the Irrawaddy river to Bhamo, are reloaded on trucks and driven up the Burma Road. (The road from Myitkyina to Tengyueh was said to be closed, though the jade workers in Tengyueh worked with jade from Burma.) When the driver put oil in our car, he did it from cans of the Burma Oil Company.

Yunnan has now only one railroad connecting it with the outside world, that between Haiphong and Kunming (built by the French), but the Chengtu–Kunming and Kweiyang–Kunming railroads are nearing completion, and the railroad from Kunming to the West is under construction. It is now being pushed ahead to Tali; in the next phase it will connect up with the Burmese railroad. This will change the trade pattern — Rangoon will be a still larger port for Chinese trade — but it keeps the old pattern from antiquity when Tacola (near Rangoon) was the seaport of the southwestern silk road.

On the Burma Road

In Tali the kanpus were insisting that the Pais and the Hans lived in harmony. They repeatedly told me that the Hueis (Moslems), the Pais, and the Hans were like brothers. The repetition of this made me doubtful. My doubt had no other foundation than their talk of harmony. Also that Tali was the only place in China where the local kanpus tried to stop Gun from taking photographs.

But it might be that my doubt was irrational, founded on a lack of understanding. To a Chinese this insistence on harmony would carry meaning. Because in China, Tali is known not only for its beauty and its marble, but also as the center of the Moslem uprising in Yunnan between 1855 and 1873. The slaughter had been done on a large scale. The wounds were deep.

Today, the Moslems constitute only 10 per cent of the Tali Pai Autonomous Chou. People's Communes have not yet been introduced. The responsible kanpus are slowly and carefully changing the social structure, and so the kanpus insist on the "Chineseness" of the Pais and the Hueis.

But there is another angle to the story. Official history in China today explains these Moslem uprisings as popular revolts against the Manchus. "Struggle against Manchu despotism and feudal exploitation and Han great-nation chauvinism." The revolt took place during the time when Great Britain was expanding over Burma, and France over Indochina. To Chinese historians today, one of the proofs of the impotence of the Ch'ing Dynasty was that it could not and would not defend the Chinese suzerainty in these countries but "abjectly signed them away." The British had made contact with the rebel Sultan of Tali; in 1871 his son went to London and from there to Turkey. This is of course treason according to the Chinese historians, and "only through an energetic attack could the Manchu troops thwart these plans." There is thus every reason to stress the harmony today.

The Chefoo Convention of 1876 gave the British (among other rights) the trade rights in Yunnan. By the agreement of 1896, "Great Britain and France agreed to share equally all privileges or advantages that might be conceded by China in the provinces of Szechuan and Yunnan."

Village near Ma Liao Pu in Upper Salween valley

Tengyueh

Going west on the Burma Road, I was reading two books I had bought in a second-hand bookshop in Kunming.One was the Kuomintang government report to the League of Nations in 1932 on "Communism in China." ("The Kuomintang has, therefore, responded adequately to the political conceptions of the Chinese people. . . . It has always professed hostility towards communism, and if in its fight against the latter it has not always achieved the success it desired, the fault was not due to the Kuomintang but to circumstances.") I found much anti-Communist literature in Chinese bookshops. The only books that seemed totally forbidden were the pornographic. The other book I read was the Whitaker's Almanack of 1910. ("With the compliments of Ilbert & Co., Shanghai, to the Customs Library, Mengtsz.")

The year 1910 is for us very far back. We might read as a quaint expression of the mood of the Europeans before World War I that: "The continued exclusiveness of the Chinese Government led by a long chain of events to the war of 1860, when British and French troops captured Peking and burnt the Summer Palace. From this date the development of foreign trade began to be most important, and for many years Great Britain's share of it was greatly predominant." But for the Chinese — any Chinese, whether in Taipeh or Peking or "overseas" — it is not a quaint expression. The memory of the decadence of the nineteenth century, when China — all under heaven — was "opened up" by the barbarians of the Far West, is still a smarting wound. This should be understood.

The building of the motor road during the war with Japan so becomes but one phase in the history of that road. The phase of "foreign dominance over the southwestern silk road, 1855–1949," as it might be called in a future Chinese history.

But Tali and the road also give another reference point for Chinese history. A.D. 751 was a year of great defeats for China. The Arab general Ziyad ibn Calid then defeated the imperial general Kao Sien-tche, and Samarkand and Balkh and all of Central Asia down to the Caspian Sea were lost to the Chinese. That year also Yunnan rose against the empire. The Chinese were beaten on both the silk roads.

Street scene, Tali

(Overleaf) The Nu Chiang (Upper Salween) valley

*Paoshan street; Jade cutter
at work, Tengyueh*

City gate of Paoshan

Tali was for some centuries the capital of an independent kingdom. Once more integrated into China, Yunnan functioned as a convenient place of deportation. Communications were bad, and many Chinese scholars and officials were exiled to Yunnan (a sort of Imperial Chinese Siberia, though with a more pleasing climate).

In Kunming we had been to a workers' club one evening. We listened to the storyteller. He was telling the end of a tale when we came in the room. He beat his drum and rattled his ivory clappers. I asked what he was reciting.

"The taking of the Loushankou pass during the Long March."

The storyteller started on a new story. I asked about it.

"An ancient story. About Wu Pao-an and his loyalty after the defeat in the southwest during the Tang Dynasty."

The audience listened with rapt attention.

Even A.D. 751 is not so far back that it is forgotten. And Tali evokes other thoughts in a Chinese than just those of marble and natural beauty. No wonder that the kanpus of Tali spoke of harmony. My doubts still tell me nothing.

We drove the road westward. Crossed the mountain ridges and rivers. They all went north–south. The road climbed and serpentined. When we had crossed the Nu river, the upper Mekong, we were stopped by a sanitation patrol. They told us that the foot-and-mouth disease was spreading from India over Burma towards Yunnan.

"The border is open to the local population. We have to spray the car, your shoes, everything. We must stop it before it goes further."

In the basins, the Han villages and cities. Higher up, minority peoples. At Paoshan the tea houses were full of people. The loudspeakers blared opera: *The Dream of the Red Chamber*. The night was filled with voices and music. Then the music changed, all the tea houses sounded the cantata to agricultural production. A man embraced me; he was drunk; he wanted to give me wine. The interpreter was ashamed of him. She said, "We Chinese are not like that."

Market life, Mangshih

Near Hsishantou the road runs across a ledge in the cliffs above the river. Suddenly we stopped. Five trucks stood in a row before us. The road was blocked. The driver ran ahead. Then he came back, laughed: "There are two cars making love."

Everybody laughed. After an hour we were rolled past the crashed cars blocking the road. Planks had been laid out. One car hung over the river far below. The driver just laughed: "The road is difficult, the traffic is heavy."

In Mangshih we lived in the kanpu hostel. Surrounded by walls. Beautiful gardens. We had passed the high mountains and the rivers. The town reminded me of Burma. To the market came the tribal people, the minorities. It was like the market in one of the Shan State towns. But no civil war.

"Our sawbwas know our strength. We give them high titles and much money. They live better now than they did as princes. Their children go to schools in Peking and Shanghai. When the old die, the young are already part of China. That is why they don't rebel as in Burma."

Mangshih had been known for malaria and bubonic plague. Now it is a moderately clean, healthy market town and administrative center.

Sitting in the Mangshih kanpu hostel garden, we were near the end of our journeys in China. Gun and I talked about what we had seen during these nine months in the most populous state in the world. I noted in my diary:

The administration functions, is honest and not corrupt. Despite local insurrections (they told me that Tunhwang in Chinghai province was "momentarily unsafe"; there is some fighting in Sinkiang and Tibet) China has not known an internal peace like this since the height of the Ming Dynasty. There is hunger but not starvation. Scarcity but no real famines. Schools, popular education, and health services have transformed the life of the people. Every career is open to the talented — though the rewards are more spiritual than material. Economically, the country is progressing.

I have read statements to the effect that China is ripe for a revolution against Peking. I don't believe it. Despite all the difficulties and mistakes, the progress is evident. And the social revolution has not "destroyed the family" (though it is changing the family along the same lines as it is being changed in Sweden). There is discontent.

"When we had the period of criticism," said one kanpu, "some peasants misunderstood it and killed the local kanpus. That was not counterrevolution. Those kanpus must have been bad. Of course, we don't propagate the idea of killing kanpus, but we distinguish between counterrevolution and the natural resentment of peasants against bad elements that have entered our ranks."

But the discontent is on a practical level. It is not directed against the system as such. I met old intellectuals who said, "It is not our way of life. It is difficult to adjust. But what other way is open for China? How can a poor country develop? Our leaders have not much choice. Can I say that I want to live in luxury, when China is poor? In the future, in one or two centuries, every Chinese will have all the material luxury he desires, if in the meanwhile we work hard, live simply. For me it is a question of morality. Should I choose my own good at the cost of China's?"

I have read much propaganda about the "immorality" of communism in China. But it is the other way around. The kanpus are as moral as the Ironsides; they are puritans and puritanical.

They came to power by the rising of the Han peasants, and they keep that power by relying on these same peasants. But in Yunnan and other outlying parts of the Chinese state, this has a double meaning. Here the Revolution came marching along the road. To the Thai villages the Revolution was brought on bayonets. And here the Chinese Revolution reaches its boundaries.

Defined by its own terms, the Revolution was to change the world: from a world of poverty, oppression, and lies to a rational world of plenty, equality, and truth. But this rationality was defined by the roots of the Revolution — the Han villages — as the rationality of the Han village.

144

Village beauties, Feng Ping village

Thai village life, Feng Ping village

149

Thus, even when the official policy towards minorities — or euphemistically, "nationalities of China" — is expressed in rational terms: respect, equality, brotherhood, the implementation of this policy is determined by the mores of the Han village. Discrimination is not allowed any longer. All are to be treated as equals, whether Hans or Thais or Lolos or Singphos. But if the marriage customs of the Singphos (among whom the girls can take lovers and change them and behave freely until married) clash with the morals of the Han village, the kanpus say, as did the intelligent Yang Su, who was leading the propaganda work in the Tehung Thai-Singpho Autonomous Chou, "In the course of the Revolution they are educated to a socialist morality, and the remnant of the former decadent morality is vanishing."

He did not answer my objection that premarital intercourse was neither revolutionary nor counterrevolutionary and that the difference between, for instance, Sweden and Switzerland in this respect could not be explained just by the possible differences in the ownership of the means of production or in political structure but had to be found in the "national traditions" and "national mores" — thus, that the policy in this case was wrong, was against the principle of respect for national differences. As far as I could see, I had only branded myself as decadent.

This is no joking matter. The Revolution could sweep over Han China like a prairie fire. Brought on bayonets by men marching the Burma Road, the sparks (kindled and fanned by trained kanpus) could slowly start a fire in the feudal (European sense) Thai area and could become a planned social transformation of the tribes living in the hills. But it could go no further. On bayonets the Chinese Revolution cannot be brought into Burma, India, and other countries.

It can give impetus, even assistance, to social change and revolution. But it loses its power as it crosses the boundary of its culture. I believe this is understood in Peking. I am not sure it is understood in the West.

Thai peasants loading sand for road construction

Plowing in Feng Ping rice fields

Village temple, Feng Ping village

It is normal for the Chinese, in defending the borders of their state, to bargain for a boundary as far out as is practical. They don't claim all the countries that have once been under Chinese suzerainty. (That would be Burma, Laos, Vietnam, Cambodia, Korea, Soviet Asia east of the Caspian Sea, North Afghanistan, etc.) I am no soothsayer, but I would be extremely surprised if China proved herself to be expansionist in this territorial sense. As surprised as if in forty years' time (granted that there had been no war finishing me off before then) I would not see a China that was the mightiest power in Asia, one of the mightiest in the world, around which — by the attraction of its mass, the power of its economy, and the ideas springing out of its example — most countries in Asia aligned themselves as iron filings in a magnetic field.

I don't want to give the impression that the kanpus in Mangshih were narrow-minded. On the contrary, they were among the most well-informed and intelligent I met in China. But even so, they could not leap over the walls crisscrossing the Han village.

China is now being unified and integrated as never before. The kanpus work hard to instill the idea of "Chineseness" — a supranational "Chineseness." Far out on the border live the Wa people. They were headhunters (for magical reasons). They accepted no state authority. The kanpus came.

"We lost some comrades," said Yang Su. "They were careless about their heads."

Changing their way of life, the kanpus praised the Wa for their headhunting: "You guarded the border of China. You kept out the imperialists. China is proud of your struggle. You proved yourselves true Chinese."

One could say that the kanpus make the transformation acceptable to the transformed by giving them pride (face) while remaking their values.

And the percentage of Han kanpus decreases as education provides local kanpus infused with the values of the Chinese Revolution to lead the further integration.

The sacrificial grove of the Santaishan Singpho village was as close to the Burmese border as I came. I looked towards the border. I had seen them from the other side before. But to see them from this side had taken me two years, and the few miles separating the two viewpoints had taken me halfway around the globe.

"But for the local people the border is open. That is the agreement. The market towns on both sides are open to the population."

The bamboo was a green curtain behind me. The posts of the spirit-gates were rotting. But the Singphos stayed away from them. Only a Han kanpu touched them. Later, I spoke with the director of the "cultural station" who led the work in the village. He was a young Singpho with his hair cut according to Chinese student fashion.

"When I was eighteen years old in 1951 . . . I volunteered to go. So I was sent to the Institute for Nationalities in Kunming. I went along the road to Kunming for fourteen days in a charcoal-burning truck. . . . I was afraid. I studied in Kunming for one year and four months. . . . Then I was selected to see our whole country. . . . We were each given a padded suit because we were going to the cold lands. . . . It took seven months and we saw Shanghai and Peking and Canton and all the big cities. When I came back, I was a changed person. . . .

"Now, I understood there was solidarity among all the peoples of China. I did not work in my own village when I came back. In the village where I worked, people refused to believe I was a Singpho. They thought I was a Han who had learned our language and our customs. But I told them of my family; my relatives came to see me. People then understood that I really was a Singpho. Some then were happy and said, 'Now we Singphos also have great men and officials.' But the chieftains said, 'You are hurting our people. You are betraying us to the Hans.' I was worried about that, but the party told me that this darkness soon would disappear and that all of us Singphos would be lifted to a high cultural standard, and afterwards I never felt any doubts. . . . We began to get our schools and to change our life and the old witchcraft disappeared. . . . I myself have married a Han girl."

Santaishan Singpho village (Singpho-Kachin)

The Disciples

In the autumn of A.D. 1884, the tenth year of Kuang Hsu, a monk from Szechuan came to Yunnanfu, the city that now is named Kunming. He was a native of Hochuan county and was called Teh Shen. He was a knowledgeable man, an artisan who could give form to the unseen. He was said to have decorated temples in his native place. The abbot of the temple called "Bamboo from Szechuan" was a fellow countryman of his. Teh Shen was there given the work of depicting the five hundred arhats.

The decorating of the temple began in 1886. Teh Shen had three disciples. They were Ling You-shen, Fey Liang, and a man who was known only as "the Dumb Monk" as he had no tongue. The master and his disciples worked for seven years. It is said that they used to go around Yunnanfu, looking for characters worth forming in clay. They built their sculptures with clay and straw over a wooden frame and painted the figures in lifelike colors.

In 1893, the holy work was finished. It was then said that several of the figures were not good enough. Also the art was not considered to be in good taste by scholars and officials. European visitors found it barbaric and devoid of real aesthetic feeling. Teh Shen then left Yunnanfu. Possibly for Szechuan. Nothing more has been heard of him. His pupil Fey Liang later made some sculptures in Chingling county, 120 li from Yunnanfu. What later happened to him is not known. A disciple of Fey Liang had been working in Anning, outside of Yunnanfu, in his youth. He was located recently as an old employee of the co-operative retail store in Kunming. It was suggested to him that he work in the cultural department of the city. But he was over sixty, and he had lost the art of his hands.

The figures have now been restored. When we saw them first, there was a group of Young Pioneers with red scarves looking at them. The leader pointed to the man with a frog and said, "That is by the master himself. You see that by the inner feeling and the delicate touch. But these are immature. Done by his pupils."

Some of the Young Pioneers had the angular faces of the Tibetan people. Most of them looked like Hans. All were serious. When they marched away, they were singing "The East Shines Red." The drum was beaten by an older boy.

Sculptures of Teh Shen, Kunming

Santaishan village school. Singpho pupil
awarded red banner of honor for fast learning

Jan Myrdal and Gun Kessle in Peking